I0813173

INSIDE THE NFL

DETROIT LIONS

by Charlie Beattie

Abdo & Daughters
MIDDLE GRADE NONFICTION

An imprint of Abdo Publishing
abdobooks.com

Published by Abdo Publishing, a division of ABDO, PO Box 398166, Minneapolis, Minnesota 55439.

Printed in China.
052025
092025

THIS BOOK CONTAINS RECYCLED MATERIALS

Cover Photos: Kevin Sabitus/Getty Images Sport/Getty Images (Jared Goff); Focus on Sport/Getty Images Sport/Getty Images (Barry Sanders)
Interior Photos: Lauren Leigh Bacho/Getty Images Sport/Getty Images, 4–5, 9, 11; Amy Lemus/NurPhoto/Getty Images, 6, 61 (top right); Kevin Sabitus/Getty Images Sport/Getty Images, 7; Steven King/Icon Sportswire/Getty Images, 8; Gregory Shamus/Getty Images Sport/Getty Images, 10; Abdo Publishing, 12–13; AP Images, 14–15, 21, 23, 32; Bettmann/Getty Images, 16, 26, 30, 33; Blackstone Studios/WGAR Broadcasting Co./Goodwill Stations Group/National Radio Personalities, 17; Mark Rucker/Transcendental Graphics/Getty Images Sport/Getty Images, 18–19; Paul Sancya/AP Images, 19, 52, 59; Lou G. Johrden/AP Images, 22; Sporting News/Getty Images, 24–25; George Gelatly/Getty Images Sport/Getty Images, 28, 29, 60 (bottom); Robert Riger/Getty Images Sport/Getty Images, 31, 60 (top); Focus on Sport/Getty Images, 34, 36, 38–39, 40, 44, 61 (bottom left); PS/AP Images, 35; Ron Galella/Ron Galella Collection/Getty Images, 37; Peter Read Miller/AP Images, 41, 63; Al Messerschmidt Archive/AP Images, 42; Getty Images Sport/Getty Images, 43; Duane Burleson/AP Images, 45, 57; Focus on Sport/Getty Images Sport/Getty Images, 46; Tom Pidgeon/AP Images, 47; Jeff Kowalsky/AFP/Getty Images, 48, 61 (top left); Betsy Peabody Rowe/Getty Images Sport/Getty Images, 49; Danny Moloshok/Getty Images Sport/Getty Images, 50–51; Al Messerschmidt/Getty Images Sport/Getty Images, 53; Morry Gash/AP Images, 54, 61 (bottom right); Detroit Lions/AP Images, 55; Nic Antaya/Getty Images Sport/Getty Images, 56; Shutterstock Images, 58

Editor: Rebecca Higgins
Series Designer: Laura Graphenteen
Production Designer: Laura Kuchar

Library of Congress Control Number: 2024948495

Publisher's Cataloging-in-Publication Data

Names: Beattie, Charlie, author.
Title: Detroit Lions / by Charlie Beattie
Description: Minneapolis, Minnesota: Abdo Publishing, 2026 | Series: Inside the NFL | Includes online resources and index.
Identifiers: ISBN 9781098296728 (lib. bdg.) | ISBN 9798384919247 (ebook)
Subjects: LCSH: Detroit Lions (Football team)--Juvenile literature. | National Football League--Juvenile literature. | Football teams--Juvenile literature. | American football--Juvenile literature.
Classification: DDC 796.333--dc23

CONTENTS

CHAPTER 1
LIONS ROAR AT LAST 4

CHAPTER 2
A MOVE TO MOTOWN 14

CHAPTER 3
TEAM OF THE DECADE 24

CHAPTER 4
THE CURSE OF BOBBY LAYNE 38

CHAPTER 5
FROM WINLESS TO WINNERS 50

TIMELINE 60
GLOSSARY 62
ONLINE RESOURCES 63
INDEX 64

Detroit Lions quarterback Jared Goff looks to make a throw on January 24, 2024.

CHAPTER 1

LIONS ROAR AT LAST

As the Detroit Lions broke the huddle, many of the 66,367 fans at Ford Field moved to the edges of their seats. Two minutes remained in the wild-card playoff game between the Lions and the Los Angeles Rams on January 14, 2024. Detroit had the ball and clung to a 24–23 lead.

The Lions needed just one more first down to finally end the team's playoff-victory drought of 32 years. It was one of the most embarrassing streaks in National Football League (NFL) history. And the Motor City was ready to celebrate. A postseason win had seemed impossible just a few years earlier.

GROWING PAINS

Detroit finished the 2020 season 5–11. It was the Lions' third consecutive losing campaign.

After the season, they hired Dan Campbell as their new head coach. He promised to give the team a new identity, but it was going to take time.

Toward the end of Dan Campbell's first season with the Lions, the team had a 0-10-1 record before finally winning its first game.

The Lions got worse before they got better. In Campbell's first year, Detroit finished 3-13-1. Lions fans could have written off the year as another failed season. But the attitude around the team felt positive. And momentum only built after Detroit finished the 2022 season 9-8. It wasn't good enough for a postseason berth, but it signaled that the Lions were on the rise.

Detroit came into 2023 with some top talent. Quarterback Jared Goff could throw to several electrifying receivers, including Amon-Ra St. Brown. Jahmyr Gibbs was one of the team's exciting running backs. The Lions' offensive line was one of football's best. Everything came together as Detroit finished 12-5 and won the National Football Conference (NFC) North Division. The Lions hadn't won a division title since 1993. Detroit looked to end another disappointing streak when the Rams came to town.

A FAST START

Detroit came out firing against Los Angeles. On the game's opening drive, Goff hit four receivers with four catches. Running back David Montgomery carried five times for 24 yards. His final touch was a 1-yard touchdown plunge to put the Lions on top.

Detroit's cheering crowd fueled the team. Gibbs added a 10-yard touchdown run late in the first quarter for a 14–3 lead. The Rams scored two touchdowns in the second quarter on long passes by former Lions star Matthew Stafford. Between Stafford's two scores, Goff added a touchdown strike of his own to rookie tight end Sam LaPorta. Detroit hung on for a 21–17 lead at halftime.

Running back Jahmyr Gibbs was one of the Lions' first-round picks in the 2023 NFL Draft.

A TENSE FINISH

Neither team found the end zone in the second half. Detroit kicker Michael Badgley drilled a 54-yard field goal early

Sam LaPorta, *left*, grabs a touchdown pass in the second quarter against the Rams.

in the third quarter to make it 24–17. But Rams kicker Brett Maher booted two field goals of his own. The Lions led 24–23 with 8:10 left in the game. They gained only 6 yards on three plays on their next drive before turning the ball over to the Rams.

To have any chance of winning, the Lions needed to stop Los Angeles. That didn't look likely when Stafford sliced the Detroit defense for a 35-yard completion. Instead, the play woke up the Lions defenders. They pushed the Rams back to third-and-14 from Detroit's 44-yard line. Then they forced Stafford to throw an incomplete pass. With 4:15 remaining, Rams coach Sean McVay decided to punt the ball back to the Lions.

If the Lions could pick up two first downs, they could run out the clock to end the game, and the city's long wait for postseason success would be over. Goff got one of them when he connected with Montgomery on an 11-yard catch on the drive's second play. Then a 1-yard rush drained the clock down to the two-minute warning.

After the timeout, Goff dropped back to pass. St. Brown broke over the middle. The sure-handed receiver caught Goff's pass and stretched beyond the first-down marker. The crowd erupted. As the clock ticked down its final seconds,

FINALLY FORD

Entering the 2023 playoffs, only two NFL teams had appeared in a playoff game at Ford Field. And neither was from Detroit. After the 2005 season, the then three-year-old stadium hosted Super Bowl XL between the Pittsburgh Steelers and the Seattle Seahawks. Pittsburgh won 21–10.

People run with flags to celebrate a Lions touchdown in 2024.

Amon-Ra St. Brown reacts after his game-sealing first-down catch.

32 years of frustration melted away in Detroit. The Lions, one of the NFL's oldest teams, had enjoyed a long and often disappointing history. But on this day, the team and its fans were ecstatic with a playoff win.

Lions defensive end Aidan Hutchinson smiles at the crowd after the team's history-making victory over the Rams in the playoffs after the 2023 season.

NFL TEAMS MAP

NFC EAST

DALLAS COWBOYS

NEW YORK GIANTS

PHILADELPHIA EAGLES

WASHINGTON COMMANDERS

NFC WEST

ARIZONA CARDINALS

LOS ANGELES RAMS

SAN FRANCISCO 49ERS

SEATTLE SEAHAWKS

NFC NORTH

CHICAGO BEARS

DETROIT LIONS

GREEN BAY PACKERS

MINNESOTA VIKINGS

NFC SOUTH

ATLANTA FALCONS

CAROLINA PANTHERS

NEW ORLEANS SAINTS

TAMPA BAY BUCCANEERS

AFC

AFC EAST

BUFFALO BILLS
MIAMI DOLPHINS
NEW ENGLAND PATRIOTS
NEW YORK JETS

AFC WEST

DENVER BRONCOS
KANSAS CITY CHIEFS
LAS VEGAS RAIDERS
LOS ANGELES CHARGERS

AFC NORTH

BALTIMORE RAVENS
CINCINNATI BENGALS
CLEVELAND BROWNS
PITTSBURGH STEELERS

AFC SOUTH

HOUSTON TEXANS

INDIANAPOLIS COLTS
JACKSONVILLE JAGUARS
TENNESSEE TITANS

Dutch Clark (7) starred for the Portsmouth Spartans and Detroit Lions during the 1930s.

CHAPTER 2

A MOVE TO MOTOWN

IN THE 1920S, THE PROFESSIONAL FOOTBALL WORLD LOOKED MUCH different than it does today. The NFL had been founded at the beginning of the decade, but the league was mostly located in the Midwestern United States. In addition to larger cities such as Chicago and Cleveland, smaller towns had NFL teams too.

There were also many semiprofessional and independent leagues. The franchise now known as the Detroit Lions got its start in one of these independent leagues. However, the team originally began in Portsmouth, Ohio. This city had housed many semipro teams through the decades. In 1928, a group of players banded together to create the Spartans. After two years of independent play, Portsmouth applied to join the NFL. Because the city was building a new stadium, its bid was accepted.

The Spartans lasted only four years in the new league, but in that short time, they managed to become a huge part of league history. Since the NFL's founding in 1920, it had not held any playoffs. Each year's champion was simply the team with the best winning percentage. However, after the 1932 season, Portsmouth and the Chicago Bears were tied in the standings. That led to a final game to determine the champion.

A vicious blizzard in Chicago forced the competition indoors. The game was played in Chicago Stadium, which was a hockey rink. This meant the field was only 60 yards long and 45 yards wide. Even worse, Portsmouth was playing without starting quarterback

The rivalry between the Lions and the Chicago Bears dates back to 1930, when the Lions were located in Portsmouth.

Dutch Clark. The Spartans' star was also the head basketball coach at Colorado College. Basketball season had started, and the school's athletic director refused to let Clark join the Spartans.

Radio executive George A. Richards bought the Lions in 1933.

Chicago won the strange game 9–0 in front of 12,000 fans, a huge crowd at the time. Because the game was so popular, the NFL had an idea. The next year, the league divided into two divisions. At the end of each season, the winners would play in an annual championship game. The Spartans' indoor defeat wasn't officially a playoff game, but it was the start of postseason NFL football.

SILVER AND BLUE

The 1933 season was the first to feature playoffs. It was also the final season for the Spartans in Portsmouth. After the team finished 6–5, George A. Richards, a radio station owner from Detroit, purchased it for $8,000. Richards moved the team to his home city. He also decided to change the name.

Detroit already had a popular baseball team nicknamed the Tigers. Richards decided on a similar nickname, the Lions. Richards hoped his team would be fierce, just like the big cats.

Richards enlisted one of his star players to help select the team's new uniform colors. Running back Glenn Presnell had been with the franchise since 1931. On Presnell's first day in Detroit, Richards pointed him to a room with several color schemes laid out. Richards told Presnell and his wife to pick which one they liked. The pair was drawn to a set of silver and blue uniforms. The Lions still wear those colors today.

TURKEY DAY

The Lions were an instant hit in the NFL. Detroit won its first 10 games in 1934 before losing to the Green Bay Packers 3–0 on

Until 1975, the Lions shared Briggs Stadium, later known as the Tiger Stadium, with the Detroit Tigers baseball team.

November 25. The Lions didn't have much time to regroup after the loss. Just four days later, they were scheduled to play the Bears. Richards laid out a scheme to draw fans from around the country. It would end up creating another NFL tradition.

To attract attention, Richards decided to schedule a Lions-Bears game on November 29, which was Thanksgiving. Since the 10-1 Lions and 11-0 Bears were two of the best teams in football, Richards went a step further. The radio mogul struck a deal with NBC to air the game nationwide. Fans from coast to coast listened to their radios as the Bears rallied in the second half for a 19-16 victory.

The loss knocked the Lions out of playoff contention. However, they brought 25,000 fans through the gates and gained notoriety around the country. Detroit played a Thanksgiving game each year through 1938. The tradition resumed in 1945 and has continued every year since.

THE INFANTRY ATTACK

Though the Lions came up short during their first NFL season, it was clear that Richards had one of the league's top teams. Detroit had a strong backfield. Dutch Clark, Ernie Caddell, and Ace Gutowsky were known as "the Infantry Attack." During the 1935 season, the trio combined for 1,173 yards on the ground and 12 of Detroit's NFL-best 15 rushing touchdowns. Each of the three backs also threw a pair of touchdown passes that season.

Lions fans deep fry a turkey before the team's Thanksgiving matchup with the Green Bay Packers in 2011.

The Lions went 2-2-1 in their first five games, then sprinted to the finish. On the final day of the season, Clark and Gutowsky each scored a rushing touchdown. Gutowsky also threw a 48-yard touchdown pass to Presnell. The Lions defeated the Brooklyn Dodgers 28–0 to claim the West Division title.

The win set up a championship matchup with the New York Giants. New York entered as the defending NFL champions, but the game was played in Detroit. Once again, the weather was a major factor. It was cold, windy, and snowing. Only 15,000 fans showed up to watch.

The Lions weren't bothered by the conditions or lack of support. Detroit had the second fewest passing attempts in the NFL, and the muddy field didn't slow down the Lions' ground game. Gutowsky finished off their opening 61-yard drive with a 2-yard touchdown run. Later in the first quarter, Clark scored on a 40-yard touchdown scamper. It was Detroit's longest play of the game and put the Lions up 13–0.

In the second quarter, the Giants' Ed Danowski threw a long touchdown pass, making the score 13–7. The game stayed that way until late in the fourth, when Detroit capitalized on a New York mistake. Danowski also served as New York's punter. With just three minutes to play, his low kick hit one of his own linemen. Detroit recovered the ball at the New York 26. Six plays later, Caddell raced around the left end for another touchdown, and Clark kicked the extra point to make it 20–7.

Ace Gutowsky, *with football*, was a key part of the Lions "Infantry Attack" backfield in the 1930s.

The Lions scored again late to round out a 26–7 victory. Just a year after moving the team, Richards was thrilled his Lions were top contenders in the NFL.

DETHRONED

Detroit's time at the top didn't last long. Despite winning at least seven games for each of the next three years, the Lions were never good enough to finish first in the competitive Western Division. Then, after the 1938 season, both Clark and Caddell retired.

Without two of their top stars, the Lions began to go downhill. Richards sold the team in 1940. In 1942, the team crumbled. Detroit finished 0–11. Many of the team's best players were fighting in World War II (1939–1945). The Lions finished the year with only five touchdowns. Quarterback Harry Hopp completed only 20 passes all year and tossed 13 interceptions. The Lions were outscored 263–38 on the season.

Fred Mandel, *far right*, purchased the Lions in 1940.

When the 1943 season rolled around, the Lions squared off with the Chicago Cardinals in the opener. Hopp scored a touchdown on a lateral. He then grabbed two touchdown receptions from the team's new quarterback, Chuck Fenenbock. Detroit won 35–17, matching its touchdown output from the entire previous season. Afterward, new owner Frank Mandel joked that it was a "great improvement." Despite the win, it would be a long time before Lions fans saw a better team on the field.

From 1943 to 1944, Frankie Sinkwich threw 19 touchdowns and 40 interceptions with the Lions.

THE CITY OF CHAMPIONS

The Lions' victory in the 1935 NFL Championship Game came as part of a great sports era for the city. The Detroit Tigers had won Major League Baseball's World Series just two months earlier. In 1936, the Detroit Red Wings won the National Hockey League's Stanley Cup. Legendary boxer Joe Louis, a Detroit native, became the heavyweight champion of the world in 1937.

In addition to being a star running back, Doak Walker also returned punts and kickoffs.

CHAPTER 3

TEAM OF THE DECADE

DETROIT STRUGGLED THROUGH THE 1940S, BUT A PAIR OF TRADES before the 1950 season revitalized the team. Quarterback Bobby Layne and running back Doak Walker had been high school teammates in the Dallas area in the 1940s. Each came to Detroit in a separate trade. Layne was a strong-armed quarterback.

Walker, who won the Heisman Trophy as college football's best player in 1948, was originally thought to be too small for the NFL. Despite a 5-foot, 11-inch, 170-pound frame, he became an instant star. In his first year with the Lions, Walker scored five rushing touchdowns and six through the air.

Detroit finished 6–6 in 1950. Before the 1951 season, the Lions promoted backfield coach Buddy Parker to head coach, mostly because they believed he could get the best out of Layne and Walker. By 1952, the Lions were a powerhouse. Detroit finished 9–3 and tied with the Los Angeles Rams for first place in the National Division. Even though Walker missed much of the year with an injury and never scored a touchdown, Layne thrived behind a strong offensive line led by tackle Lou Creekmur. On defense, safeties Bob Smith and Jack Christiansen had a combined total of 11 interceptions.

The Lions and the Rams had to play a tiebreaker playoff to see who would face the Cleveland Browns in the championship game. By that time, Walker had returned. His 24-yard touchdown pass to Leon Hart was a key play in Detroit's 31–21 victory.

Bobby Layne (22) and the Lions were a powerhouse in the 1950s.

A BORDER RIVALRY

The Lions had defeated the Browns 17–6 during the regular season. Both Smith and Christiansen had intercepted Cleveland's star quarterback, Otto Graham. Layne had backed them up by throwing two touchdown passes to Hart.

In the rematch for the championship, Layne broke a scoreless tie with a 2-yard touchdown run in the second quarter. The Lions still led 7–0 early in the third quarter. On a second-down play from Detroit's 33, Walker took a handoff from Layne and sprinted up the middle. After breaking two tackles, he outraced the Cleveland defense for a 67-yard touchdown.

Walker's only touchdown of the season was the biggest play in Detroit's 17–7 victory, clinching the team's second league championship. And the rivalry between the two neighboring teams was just heating up.

In 1953, the 11–1 Browns and the 10–2 Lions met again in the championship game at Detroit's Briggs Stadium. During the first half, Walker's short touchdown run and field goal put Detroit up 10–3. But the Lions' offense was shut down from there. Layne and his team found themselves down 16–10 with just over four minutes left. The Lions took over at their own 20-yard line, and Layne smoothly moved the team down the field.

With under a minute left, Layne dropped back from the Cleveland 33-yard line. Receiver Jim Doran broke open behind a defender on the right sideline, and Layne lobbed a perfect pass for the tying touchdown. Walker added the extra point to put the Lions ahead. An interception sealed the 17–16 win. Detroit became just the third team since 1933, when the NFL began playing championship games, to win back-to-back titles.

No team had won three consecutive championships since the Green Bay Packers in the pre-title game era of 1929 through 1931. Detroit certainly looked like a team that could repeat as champion after finishing 9-2-1 in 1954. On the final day of the regular season, the Lions knocked off the Browns 14–10. The two teams met again a week later to decide the champion.

This time, nothing went right for Detroit. Layne threw six interceptions. Walker touched the ball only five times on offense, totaling 52 yards. Cleveland routed the Lions 56–10 to end Detroit's dreams of a three-peat.

A pair of Detroit defenders takes down Cleveland Browns quarterback Otto Graham in the 1952 NFL Championship game.

THE COMEBACK

After the crushing defeat in the 1954 title game, Detroit slumped to 3–9 in 1955. Walker retired after that season at just 28 years old to focus on his businesses in Texas. Then, just two days before the start of the 1957 preseason, Parker quit as head coach over his frustrations with the team's owners.

All signs indicated that the team's potential dynasty was officially over. It seemed especially true after Layne broke his ankle in the second to last game of the 1957 regular season. New coach George Wilson had been rotating between Layne and Tobin Rote at quarterback. Now Rote was left to lead Detroit by himself. The Lions finished with an 8–4 record, which tied the San Francisco 49ers for first place in the West Division standings.

The Lions and 49ers met at Kezar Stadium in San Francisco to decide who would advance to the championship game. After the first half, Detroit looked finished. The 49ers held a 24–7 lead. San Francisco had already printed tickets

Lions players carry coach Buddy Parker off the field after the Lions claimed another championship in 1953.

for the championship game to be played a week later.

As the teams regrouped in their locker rooms, the Lions players could hear the 49ers laughing and celebrating through the wall separating the two rooms. Wilson, who had been planning a big speech, instead turned to his team and said, "That's what they think of you."

Bobby Layne threw for more than 15,000 yards in his career with the Lions.

The 49ers upped the score to 27–7 on the second half's opening drive. Then an unexpected hero stepped up for Detroit. Second-year fullback Tom Tracy entered the game with only 78 career rushing yards and zero touchdowns. He hadn't even touched the ball in the previous four games. But in the third quarter, he kick-started the team's comeback with a 1-yard touchdown run. Just over a minute later, Tracy ripped off a 58-yard score to cut the lead to 27–21.

"THAT'S WHAT THEY THINK OF YOU."

—GEORGE WILSON

Detroit finished off the comeback in the fourth quarter when halfback Gene Gedman scored on a 2-yard run. Lions kicker Jim Martin added a short field goal and sealed the team's 31–27 victory over the 49ers. The incredible comeback sent the Lions back to the championship game. For the fourth time in the decade, they would battle Cleveland for the title.

THE TRADE

Early in the season, Rote split time with Layne at quarterback. Then he started five games. However, Rote had been quietly good all year. And he saved his best performance for the championship rematch with the Browns.

George Wilson, *center*, coached the Lions from 1957 to 1964.

By the end of the first quarter, both Rote and Gedman had rushed for touchdowns to help Detroit build a quick 17–0 lead. At the end of the first half, it was 31–7. Rote threw one touchdown in the second quarter, then added three more after halftime. The highlight was a 78-yard bomb to Doran in the third quarter. Detroit made a commanding 59–14 victory. Though the Browns and Lions had each dominated the NFL in the 1950s, Detroit had claimed its third title against Cleveland. However, those good times were about to end.

Early in the 1958 season, the Lions made a shocking move. Though Rote had just put in a stellar performance in the championship game, many Lions still considered Layne the heart of the team. After Layne struggled through the first two games of the

Tobin Rote, *left*, smiles in the locker room after leading the Lions to the 1957 NFL championship.

Yale Lary played 11 seasons with the Lions from 1952 to 1964.

season, Wilson decided to trade the veteran quarterback to the woeful Pittsburgh Steelers. His teammates were shocked. The 1958 season quickly went downhill, with the Lions winning only four games.

It was later rumored that Layne was traded because he had been gambling on Lions games, though that was never proved. What was

Alex Karras (71) led a fierce Lions defense in the 1950s and 1960s.

true is that the star quarterback was furious. Supposedly, as he left the Lions locker room he told his teammates that Detroit wouldn't win another title for 50 years. That story was never verified either, but "the Curse of Bobby Layne" was born.

At the start of the 1960s, Detroit didn't look like a cursed team. In fact, the Lions seemed ready to compete for titles once again.

Though they no longer had a star quarterback, the Lions had a stellar defense. Linebacker Joe Schmidt had been a standout for the team since 1953. His strong play earned him the nickname "Mr. Detroit Lion."

Up front, Schmidt was joined by defensive tackle Alex Karras. The lineman missed only one game because of injury in his 13-year career while also dabbling in both professional wrestling and acting. In the secondary, Dick "Night Train" Lane joined the Lions in 1960. He piled up 20 interceptions in his first four seasons in Detroit.

The stout defense helped Detroit to seven wins in 1960, eight in 1961, and 11 a year later. The 1962 Lions never trailed by more than a touchdown in any game. However, at the time the NFL postseason was still just a single game between division champions. As good as the Lions were, they could not get past their division's dominant Packers. While Green Bay played for championships, the Lions had to settle for the NFL's new

Dick "Night Train" Lane goes up for an interception in a game against the Baltimore Colts.

The Green Bay Packers often stopped the Lions in the early 1960s.

third-place game, which was known as the Playoff Bowl. Detroit had won the bowl two years in a row. After the 1962 season, the team faced Layne's Pittsburgh Steelers. Lions defensive back Yale Lary sealed the 17–10 win by intercepting Layne in the final minute.

A NEW RECRUIT

The Lions had an unusual invite to their 1963 training camp. Writer George Plimpton wanted to explain to readers how hard it was to make an NFL team. The Lions allowed him to try out as a third-string quarterback. Plimpton appeared for only four plays of a team scrimmage, none of which gained yards. He turned his experience into a series of *Sports Illustrated* articles, and he later compiled them into a best-selling book called *Paper Lion: Confessions of a Last-String Quarterback*. The book was later made into a 1968 film.

George Plimpton shows his Lions spirit in 1991.

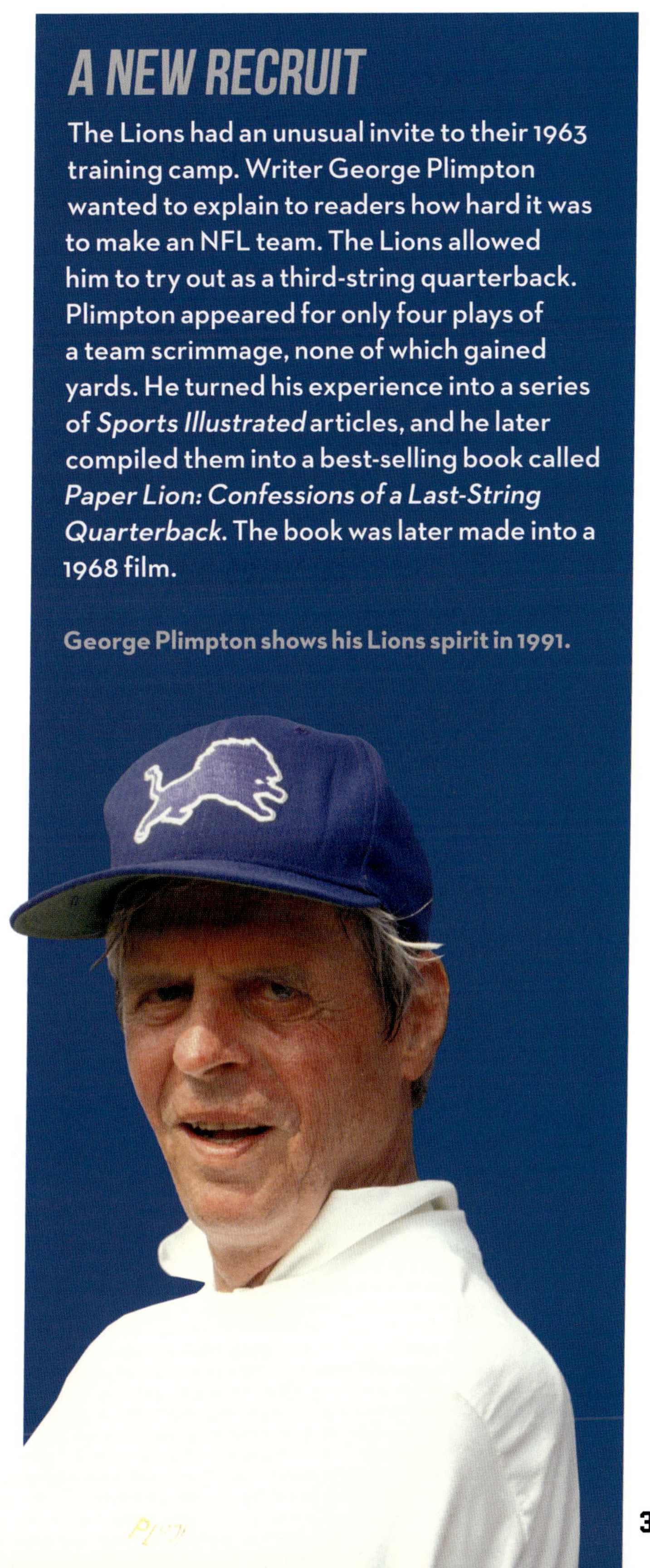

Lem Barney, *right*, intercepted 56 passes in his 11 years with the Detroit Lions after joining the team in 1967.

CHAPTER 4

THE CURSE OF BOBBY LAYNE

In 1960, the American Football League (AFL) was created. The new league attempted to compete with the more established NFL. After six years, the leagues decided to combine under the NFL name. Lions linebacker Joe Schmidt retired before the merger. But he returned to the team as a linebacker coach. In 1967, he was promoted to head coach.

Three years later, in 1970, the AFL and NFL merger became official. As part of the merger, the 26-team league expanded its playoffs. In 1970, Schmidt's Lions finished in second place for the second straight year. They would later extend their second-place streak to a total of seven seasons. But the 1970 Lions' 10–4 record was good enough for a brand-new wild-card playoff spot.

The good news ended there. Detroit put on a poor playoff display. Competing against the Dallas Cowboys on the road, the Lions mustered only 156 yards in a strange 5–0 loss. It was the lowest scoring postseason game in NFL history.

Quarterback Greg Landry threw for only 48 yards, was sacked three times, and fumbled twice in Detroit's 5–0 playoff loss to Dallas in 1970.

NEW HOME, NEW STAR

In 1975, the Lions took the field inside of the NFL's newest and biggest stadium. The Pontiac Silverdome held more than 80,000 people. The stadium in suburban Detroit was also one of only two fully indoor fields in the league.

With many seats to fill, the Lions needed a star attraction. They found one after finishing 2–14 in 1979. The Lions used their first overall pick in the 1980 draft on Heisman Trophy-winning running back Billy Sims of Oklahoma.

The 6-foot, 212-pound Sims was a powerful runner, and he took the NFL by storm. In his rookie season, Sims led the NFL with 13 rushing touchdowns and 16 total touchdowns while piling up 1,303 yards. Even better, the running back helped the Lions improve their standing. Detroit reached the playoffs in 1982 in a strike-shortened season. A year later, the 9–7 Lions won the NFC Central Division. Sims was a commanding force, leading the team with 1,040 rushing yards and seven touchdowns despite missing three games.

The Lions traveled to face the San Francisco 49ers in the divisional round of the playoffs. Sims did his part, rushing for 114 yards on 20 carries. That helped overcome five interceptions thrown by Detroit quarterback Gary Danielson. In the fourth quarter, Sims scored twice to erase a 17–9 deficit. However, 49ers star quarterback Joe Montana threw a touchdown pass to secure a late 24–23 lead.

Danielson managed to maneuver the Lions into field-goal range with 11 seconds left. Earlier in the game, Detroit kicker Eddie Murray had booted a playoff-record 54-yarder.

Billy Sims was an instant star for Detroit, rushing for 153 yards and three touchdowns in his first game.

With the game on the line, Murray missed a 43-yard attempt wide to the right, and the Lions' playoff curse continued.

BARRY SANDERS

Sims's time in the NFL came to a crashing halt on October 21, 1984. Playing against the Minnesota Vikings, he suffered a devastating knee injury. Despite two years trying to rehabilitate his damaged knee, Sims never played in the NFL again.

Without their star, the Lions declined. In 1988, Detroit finished 4–12, which gave it the number three pick in the 1989 draft. Once again, the Lions picked a running back who had won the Heisman Trophy. Barry Sanders claimed the prize while playing for Sims's rival school, Oklahoma State.

Sanders even adopted Sims's beloved No. 20 uniform. The new back quickly showed he was worthy of the number. In his introductory press conference, Sanders talked about

Eddie Murray was the Lions' kicker from 1980 to 1991.

Sims looks for open space during the Lions' divisional playoff game against the San Francisco 49ers after the 1983 season.

wanting to bring back the cheering crowds in the Silverdome. He said, "It's a privilege to be one of the players that will help restore the roar."

> **"IT'S A PRIVILEGE TO BE ONE OF THE PLAYERS THAT WILL HELP RESTORE THE ROAR."**
>
> **—BARRY SANDERS**

In Week 1 of the 1989 season, the Detroit crowd was roaring for Sanders even before he got the ball in his first game. He finally took the field in the second half. On his first professional carry, Sanders sprinted 18 yards before

From the moment he took to an NFL field in 1989, Barry Sanders (20) was one of the most exciting players in the league.

three Phoenix Cardinals wrestled him to the turf. Sanders ended the game with 71 yards and a touchdown.

The cheers of Lions fans only increased, as the 5-foot-8-inch, 203-pound Sanders was one of the must-see players in the NFL. His runs became legendary, full of impossibly quick cuts and magician-like escapes. It wasn't uncommon to see Sanders stopped by a swarm of defenders, only to somehow wriggle free for even more yards.

Though Sanders was electric on the field, he was decidedly low-key. In an era when big, flashy celebrations were becoming normal, Sanders simply tossed the ball to an official and returned to the sideline after scoring. The humble star cared little for records. On the final day of his rookie season, Sanders passed up the chance to overtake Christian Okoye of the Kansas City Chiefs for the league rushing lead. He only needed a handful of yards. But in the closing minutes, Sanders stayed on the sidelines because the game was already won.

With their incredible running back, the Lions became a playoff team again. In 1991, Sanders scored an NFL-best 16 touchdowns and led Detroit to a 12–4 record, the most wins in team history. Having clinched a division title, Detroit hosted Dallas in the divisional round.

Despite being held in check all game, Sanders still managed to steal the headlines in a 38–6 blowout win. On second-and-10 from the Cowboys' 47 late in the fourth quarter,

Sanders's incredible lower-body strength made him tough to tackle and able to change direction quickly.

Sanders took a handoff and ran to the right. He was met head-on by a Dallas defender 6 yards upfield. Sanders bounced off the collision, then he quickly weaved through a handful of other defenders before sprinting to the end zone. The iconic touchdown sewed up Detroit's first significant postseason win since the 1957 season.

Lions fans were optimistic that Sanders and his teammates could end Bobby Layne's curse. The team traveled to Washington for the NFC title game. But Sanders touched the ball only 15 times. He had 15 receiving yards and gained 44 yards. Washington jumped out to an early lead. Quarterbacks Erik Kramer and Andre Ware were unable to bring the Lions back, and they were defeated 38–10.

Wayne Fontes coached the Lions from 1988 to 1996. His 66 victories were the most in team history at the time.

The Lions had inconsistent quarterbacks for the rest of the decade. While Sanders remained one of the NFL's most watchable players, he rarely had the help he needed

Scott Mitchell was one of many quarterbacks the Lions used in the 1990s to try and help Barry Sanders.

from teammates to make Detroit a winning team. The Lions reached the playoffs after the 1993, 1994, and 1995 seasons but lost in the wild-card round each time.

SANDERS EXITS

Sanders had a slow start to the 1997 season, rushing for only 53 yards in his first two games and had 102 receiving yards in the second game. For the rest of the year, he was phenomenal. Starting with a 161-yard performance against the Bears in Week 3, Sanders ripped off 14 straight 100-yard efforts. Twice during that stretch, he topped 200 yards.

Entering the final day of the season at home against the New York Jets, Sanders needed 131 rushing yards to reach 2,000 for the season. Only two backs had ever accomplished the feat.

Sanders is carried off the field at the Pontiac Silverdome after breaking the 2,000-yard barrier in the final game of the 1997 season.

When the Jets held Sanders to 20 yards in the first half, it looked as if Sanders might not make it.

On the last play of the third quarter, he finally broke a big gain of 47 yards. Two carries later, he scored the Lions' only touchdown of the day to give the team a 13–10 lead. With a 2-yard gain late in the fourth, Sanders reached exactly 2,000.

But he kept going. On the next play, Sanders broke open for 53 yards. Only one player had ever rushed for more than Sanders's 2,053 yards at the time. The Lions' win also earned them a trip to the playoffs. However, their postseason run ended the following week with a 20–11 loss to the Tampa Bay Buccaneers.

In the 1998 season, Sanders rushed for more than 1,400 yards. That left him fewer than 1,500 yards shy of the NFL record. At 30 years old, Sanders appeared certain to become the league's all-time leading rusher, maybe as soon as 1999. Instead, he shocked football fans everywhere by suddenly retiring. He remains beloved in Detroit, but fans also wonder what might have been if he kept playing. Instead, the Lions were starting over again.

THUMBS UP

On November 17, 1991, Lions center Mike Utley blocked a Los Angeles Rams defender. The defender fell on Utley's head and neck. Utley was unable to move. While medical personnel carried Utley off the field at the Silverdome, he gave a thumbs-up gesture to the crowd. At the hospital, Utley was told he was paralyzed. The Lions rallied around him, and the thumbs-up became Detroit's symbol for their 1991 playoff run.

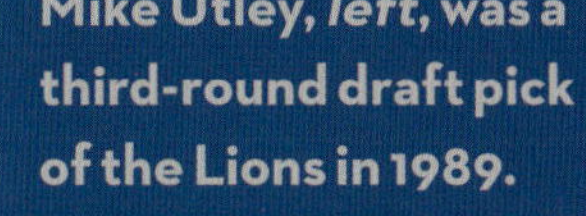

Mike Utley, *left*, was a third-round draft pick of the Lions in 1989.

Running back James Stewart (34) carries the ball against the Minnesota Vikings in the Lions' first win of the 2001 season.

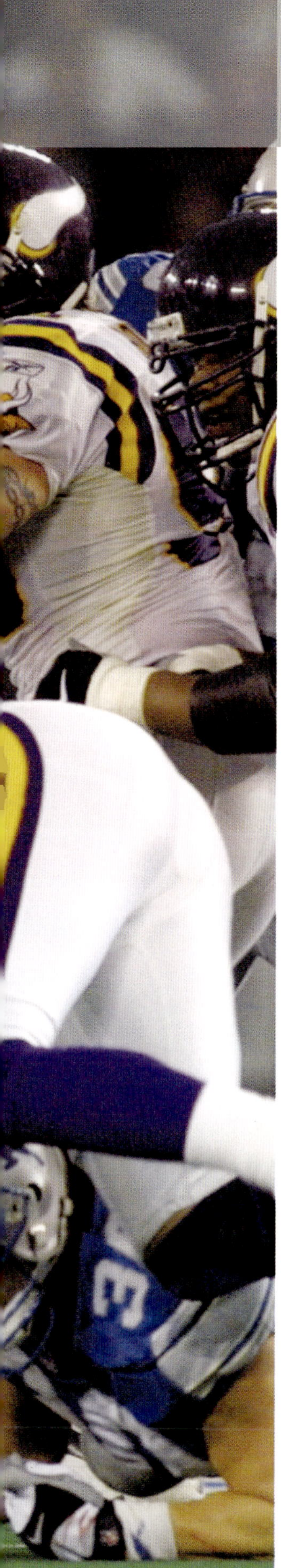

CHAPTER 5

FROM WINLESS TO WINNERS

The Lions hung on in their first two seasons without Barry Sanders. Detroit even made the playoffs in 1999 with an 8–8 record. However, the Lions once again lost in the wild-card round. In 2000, the Lions improved to 9–7, but that wasn't good enough to reach the postseason.

The bottom fell out in 2001. Under first-year head coach Marty Mornhinweg, Detroit lost its first 12 games. No team had gone winless in a season since the NFL had moved to a 16-game schedule in 1978. The Lions looked as if they might be the first.

They blew a 20–7 lead in Week 13 against the Minnesota Vikings. Only a 1-yard touchdown run by Detroit fullback Corey Schlesinger with 10:36 left saved the victory. The Lions managed to finish the season 2–14. But big changes were needed, especially with the Lions set to move into a new home, Ford Field, in 2002.

Longtime team owner William Clay Ford approached Matt Millen to become Detroit's general manager. The former linebacker retired after winning four Super Bowls. He went on to become a respected television broadcaster. However, he had never run a team and told Ford he didn't think he was qualified. Ford hired him anyway.

The results were a disaster. Detroit didn't win a road game in any of Millen's first three seasons. The young team was consistently overmatched on the field.

In the 2002 draft, Millen took quarterback Joey Harrington over several future stars. Harrington lasted only four poor years in Detroit. In each of the next three drafts, Millen took wide receivers in the first round. Only one, 2004 draft pick Roy Williams, turned out to be a solid player.

Matt Millen selected receivers Roy Williams (11), Mike Williams (88), and Charles Rogers (80) in consecutive drafts. These athletes struggled in the NFL.

0–16

By the 2008 season, the Lions were a mess. The team's five quarterbacks that year had a combined total of 18 touchdowns and 19 interceptions. Running back Kevin Smith had a solid season, rushing for 976 yards and scoring eight times. But the rest of the offense ran for only two touchdowns all year. Meanwhile, the defense allowed 517 points, which at the time was the second most in an NFL season ever.

The Lions had a 31–84 record during Millen's eight years with the team.

Millen was fired after Detroit suffered three lopsided defeats to start the 2008 season. In Week 6, the Lions were on the road at Minnesota and lost 12–10 on a late field goal. However, the difference in the game turned out to be a comical safety taken by quarterback Dan Orlovsky. In the first quarter, he was being chased by a Vikings defensive lineman in his own end zone. Forgetting where he was on the field, Orlovsky stepped out of the back of the end zone without being touched.

In the final week of the season, the Lions traveled to take on the Green Bay Packers. With a dubious record on the line, the Lions made history in more ways than one. Detroit became the first team to allow two 100-yard rushers and two 100-yard receivers in the same game. The 31–21 defeat also made the Lions the first team to finish 0–16.

MEGATRON AND MATT

Though the 2008 Lions were mostly a punchline, they did have one incredible player on their roster. Wide receiver Calvin Johnson had been Detroit's top pick in the 2007 NFL Draft. The 6-foot, 5-inch receiver had a tight end's frame at 237 pounds. But he also had incredible speed, great leaping ability, and soft hands. His combination of skills earned him the nickname "Megatron," which came from a powerful Transformers character.

Even as the Lions were winless, Johnson broke out with an NFL-best 12 touchdown catches in 2008. With the top pick in the 2009 draft, the Lions selected quarterback Matthew Stafford of Georgia. Though Johnson had played for Stafford's archrival Georgia Tech, the two soon became a dangerous passing duo in Detroit.

However, it took until 2011 for the pair to really

Quarterback Dan Orlovsky walks off the field after the Lions' final loss of their winless 2008 season.

break out. Stafford struggled as a 21-year-old rookie in 2009. But by 2011, he and Johnson were among the league's best players, and it showed on the field. In Week 2, Stafford threw two of his four touchdown passes to Johnson as the Lions beat the Kansas City Chiefs 48–3. It was the largest margin of victory in Detroit history.

Calvin Johnson's combination of size and agility made him one of the most dangerous weapons in the NFL.

That win helped fuel the team's first 5–0 start since 1956. After an up-and-down stretch in the middle of the season, the Lions clinched a playoff berth with a win over the San Diego Chargers in Week 16. Stafford also broke the team record for passing yards in a season in the 38–10 victory. After the game, Stafford led a victory lap around Ford Field, high-fiving fans who had been waiting since the 1999 season to reach the playoffs again. Once again, Detroit's postseason didn't last long. Against the New Orleans Saints, Detroit's defense allowed 626 yards of offense, a playoff record at the time. The Lions lost 45–28.

Even with two superstars, the Lions remained inconsistent for years. After the 2014 season, Detroit went to Dallas and built a 14–0 lead over the Cowboys in the wild-card round. However, Dallas scored on a late touchdown pass to seal a 24–20 comeback win.

Matthew Stafford throws during the Lions' record-setting win over the Kansas City Chiefs in 2011.

Johnson played only one more season. Like Sanders, he retired at 30 years old, leaving Lions fans wanting more. Stafford struggled on. The quarterback became beloved in Detroit for his ability to play through defensive punishment. He led Detroit back to the postseason in 2016. But as had happened so many times before, the Lions bowed out in the wild-card round.

BITING KNEECAPS

Just as the Lions had shuffled through players throughout the 2000s, they also churned through coaches. From 2000 through 2020, the Lions went through nine head coaches. After a 5–11 season in 2020, Detroit was again looking for a new boss.

The team hired Dan Campbell, a former tight end who had played three seasons with the Lions. Campbell had only 12 games of head coaching experience, finishing 5–7 at the helm of the Miami Dolphins in 2015. He was a respected player for his toughness, and he vowed to bring that to Detroit. At his opening press conference, Campbell memorably said, "We're going to kick you in the teeth, all right, and when you punch us back, we're going to smile at you. And when you knock us down, we're going to get up, and on the way up, we're going to bite a kneecap off."

"AND WHEN YOU KNOCK US DOWN, WE'RE GOING TO GET UP, AND ON THE WAY UP, WE'RE GOING TO BITE A KNEECAP OFF."

—DAN CAMPBELL

Many coaches had promised to change Detroit's losing culture. But Campbell's fighting words showed fans he was serious. The team soon put together a solid group on the field. But it was without Stafford, who was traded to the Los Angeles Rams after the 2020 season. In return, the Lions got former top pick Jared Goff. The quarterback had led the Rams to the Super Bowl after the 2018 season. Around Goff, the Lions built a tough offensive line led by center Frank Ragnow and tackle Penei Sewell. Detroit found a steal in the 2021 draft, selecting exciting receiver Amon-Ra St. Brown in the fourth round. A year later, Detroit drafted Michigan native Aidan Hutchinson with its top pick. The homegrown defensive end quickly turned into a team leader.

With talent on the field, the Lions steadily got better. In Campbell's second season, Detroit improved from three wins to nine. But the Lions finally broke through in 2023. Playing at home on the final day of the season, a reenergized Goff hit St. Brown on a

SALUTE TO STAFFORD

Lions fans didn't stop cheering for Matthew Stafford after he was traded in 2020. When Stafford won the Super Bowl with the Rams a year later, he thanked Detroit in a post-game interview. Many fans and former Lions teammates flooded social media with praise and celebration for Stafford's win.

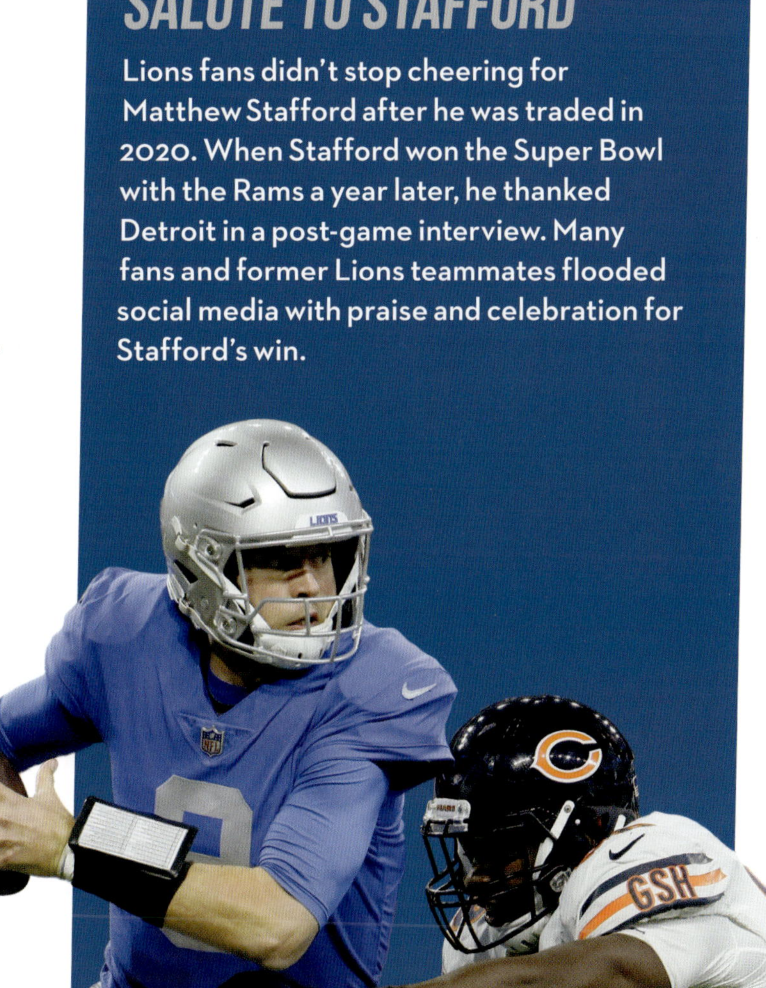

LIONS TROPHY CASE

SUPER BOWL CHAMPIONSHIPS: 0

NFL CHAMPIONSHIPS: 4

1935, 1952, 1953, 1957

CONFERENCE CHAMPIONSHIPS: 4

NFL National: 1952
NFL West: 1953, 1954, 1957

DIVISION TITLES: 5

NFL West: 1935
NFC Central: 1983, 1991, 1993
NFC North: 2023, 2024

All stats are through the 2024 season.

70-yard touchdown pass 15 seconds into the fourth quarter against the Vikings. The highlight play was a bonus to the Lions, who had already clinched the division.

Detroit outlasted Stafford's Rams in the wild-card round for its first playoff victory since January 1992. Goff then threw two touchdown passes in the divisional round to knock out the Tampa Bay Buccaneers. Suddenly the Lions were one step from the Super Bowl.

The Lions raced out to a 24–7 halftime lead over the San Francisco 49ers in the NFC title game. But the 49ers came storming back in the second half on their home turf. San Francisco escaped with a 34–31 victory.

The Lions remained the only team that had existed for each year of the Super Bowl era that had yet to play in football's ultimate game. But the 2024 team looked like it might break through. Detroit finished 15–2 behind a stellar offense that scored a franchise-record 564 points. The Lions were the top seed heading into the NFC playoffs. But by the divisional round, the Lions' defense had suffered multiple injuries. They were unable to stop the underdog Washington Commanders and lost 45–31. Though the championship dream felt closer than ever for Lions fans, they would have to wait and hope for at least another year.

Amon-Ra St. Brown hauls in a touchdown pass in Detroit's divisional playoff matchup against the Tampa Bay Buccaneers in January 2024.

TIMELINE

1928
The Portsmouth Spartans are formed in Portsmouth, Ohio.

1934
The Spartans move to Detroit and are renamed the Lions by owner George A. Richards. That same year, Detroit plays its first Thanksgiving game.

1935
The Lions win their first NFL championship by defeating the New York Giants 26-7 behind stars Dutch Clark and Ernie Caddell.

1952
Detroit wins its first NFL title in 17 years by beating the rival Cleveland Browns 17-7.

1953
The Lions repeat as champions when Layne hits Jim Doran on a 33-yard touchdown pass late in the game to give Detroit a 17-16 victory over Cleveland.

1954
Detroit reaches the championship game for the third consecutive season but falls 56-10 to the Browns.

1957
Detroit rallies from 27-7 down against the San Francisco 49ers in a playoff game to win 31-27. The Lions then rout the Browns 59-14 to win their third championship of the decade.

1970
The Lions reach the playoffs for the first time since Layne was traded, but they fall 5–0 in the divisional round to the Dallas Cowboys.

1983
The Lions fall just short against the 49ers in the divisional playoffs when kicker Eddie Murray misses a potential game-winning field goal in the final minute.

1991
Behind star running back Barry Sanders, the Lions win the NFC Central Division and capture their first playoff win since 1957 by beating the Dallas Cowboys 38–6.

1997
Sanders becomes just the third running back to rush for more than 2,000 yards in a season.

2008
The Lions finish 0–16, becoming the first winless NFL team since the 16-game schedule was adopted.

2023
Led by Dan Campbell and quarterback Jared Goff, the Lions reach the NFC title game, but they lose to San Francisco 34–31.

2024
The Lions finish 15–2 behind the best offense in team history, but are upset in the divisional playoffs.

GLOSSARY

athletic director–the person in charge of an athletic department at a college or university.

clinch–when a team secures something, such as a win or a playoff berth.

draft–a system that allows teams to acquire new players coming into a league.

dynasty–a team that has an extended period of success, usually winning multiple championships in the process.

franchise–an entire sports organization.

general manager–an executive who runs a team and is responsible for finding and signing players.

iconic–well-known for excellence.

interception–a pass that is caught by a defensive player.

lateral–a pass that goes sideways or backward.

merger–joining one thing with another to create something new, such as a company, a team, or a league.

momentum–the strength or force that allows something to continue or to grow stronger.

postseason–another word for playoffs; the time after the end of the regular season when teams play to determine a champion.

professional–a person who gets paid to perform.

retire–to end one's career.

rival–an opponent with whom a player or team has a fierce and ongoing competition.

rookie–a professional athlete in his or her first year of competition.

scheme—a set of formations that a team regularly uses.

secondary—the defensive players—cornerbacks and safeties—who start the play farthest from the line.

semiprofessional—something that pays, but not well enough to make a living.

veteran—someone who has played for many years.

ONLINE RESOURCES

To learn more about the Detroit Lions, please visit **abdobooklinks.com** or scan this QR code. These links are routinely monitored and updated to provide the most current information available.

INDEX

B

Badgley, Michael, 7-8
Briggs Stadium, 27

C

Caddell, Ernie, 20, 21, 22
Campbell, Dan, 6, 56-57
Chicago Bears, 16-17, 19-20, 47
Christiansen, Jack, 26, 27
Clark, Dutch, 17, 20-21, 22
Cleveland Browns, 26, 27, 28, 30, 31-32
Creekmur, Lou, 26

D

Dallas Cowboys, 40, 45-46, 55
Danielson, Gary, 41
Danowski, Ed, 21
Doran, Jim, 27, 32

F

Fenenbock, Chuck, 23
Ford, William Clay, 52
Ford Field, 5, 9, 52, 55

G

Gedman, Gene, 30, 32
Gibbs, Jahmyr, 6
Goff, Jared, 6, 7, 9, 57, 59
Graham, Otto, 27
Green Bay Packers, 18, 28, 35, 53
Gutowsky, Ace, 20-21

H

Harrington, Joey, 52
Hart, Leon, 26, 27
Heisman Trophies, 25, 40, 42
Hopp, Harry, 22-23
Hutchinson, Aidan, 57

J

Johnson, Calvin, 54-56

K

Kansas City Chiefs, 45, 55
Karras, Alex, 35
Kramer, Erik, 46

L

Lane, Dick, 35
LaPorta, Sam, 7
Lary, Yale, 37
Layne, Bobby, 25-26, 27-28, 29, 31, 32-34, 37, 46
Los Angeles Rams, 5, 7, 8-9, 26, 49, 57-59

M

Maher, Brett, 8
Mandel, Frank, 23
Martin, Jim, 30
McVay, Sean, 9
Miami Dolphins, 56
Millen, Matt, 52, 53
Minnesota Vikings, 42, 51, 53, 57
Montana, Joe, 41
Montgomery, David, 7, 9
Mornhinweg, Marty, 51
Murray, Eddie, 41-42

N

New Orleans Saints, 55
New York Giants, 20-21
New York Jets, 47-48

O

Okoye, Christian, 45
Orlovsky, Dan, 53

P

Parker, Buddy, 25-26, 29
Pittsburgh Steelers, 9, 33, 37
Plimpton, George, 37
Presnell, Glenn, 18, 20

R

Ragnow, Frank, 57
Richards, George A., 17-18, 19-20, 22
Rote, Tobin, 29, 31-32

S

San Diego Chargers, 55
San Francisco 49ers, 29-30, 41, 59
Sanders, Barry, 42-49, 51, 56
Schlesinger, Corey, 51
Schmidt, Joe, 35, 39
Seattle Seahawks, 9
Sewell, Penei, 57
Sims, Billy, 40-41, 42
Smith, Bob, 26, 27
Smith, Kevin, 53
St. Brown, Amon-Ra, 6, 9, 57
Stafford, Matthew, 7, 8-9, 54-56, 57, 59
Super Bowls, 9, 52, 57, 59

T

Tampa Bay Buccaneers, 49, 59
Tracy, Tom, 30

U

Utley, Mike, 49

W

Walker, Doak, 25-26, 27-28, 29
Ware, Andre, 46
Williams, Roy, 52
Wilson, George, 29-30, 33